COMPLETE
VIOLIN SONATAS

LUDWIG VAN BEETHOVEN

FROM THE BREITKOPF & HÄRTEL
COMPLETE WORKS EDITION

D1603939

Dover Publications, Inc., New York

Published in Canada by General Publishing Company, Ltd.,
30 Lesmill Road, Don Mills, Toronto, Ontario.
Published in the United Kingdom by Constable and Company, Ltd.

This Dover edition, first published in 1990, is a
republication of a portion of Series 12 ("Für Pianoforte und Violine")
from the collection *Ludwig van Beethoven's Werke. Vollständige
kritisch durchgesehene überall berechtigte Ausgabe. Mit
Genehmigung aller Originalverleger*, published by Breitkopf
& Härtel, Leipzig, n.d. We are grateful to the
Music Library at Wellesley College for
the loan of the score.

Manufactured in the United States of America
Dover Publications, Inc.
31 East 2nd Street
Mineola, N.Y. 11501

Library of Congress Cataloging-in-Publication Data

Beethoven, Ludwig van, 1770–1827.
[Sonatas, violin, piano]
Complete violin sonatas.

"From the Breitkopf & Härtel complete works edition."
1. Sonatas (Violin and piano)—Scores. I. Title.
M219.B416B77 1990   89-29970
ISBN 0-486-26277-4

Contents

Violin Sonata No. 1 in D Major

OP. 12, NO. 1

1

2

TEMA con VARIAZIONI.

Andante con moto.

VAR.1.

VAR. 3.
Minore.

RONDO.

Allegro.

Violin Sonata No. 2 in A Major

OP. 12, NO. 2

26   *Violin Sonata No. 2*

Andante, più tosto Allegretto.

Andante, più tosto Allegretto.

Violin Sonata No. 3 in E-flat Major

OP. 12, NO. 3

44   *Violin Sonata No. 3*

RONDO.
Allegro molto.

Violin Sonata No. 4 in A Minor

OP. 23

Violin Sonata No. 5 in F Major ("Spring")

OP. 24

84   *Violin Sonata No. 5*

86   *Violin Sonata No. 5*

SCHERZO.

Allegro molto.

Allegro molto.
La prima parte senza repetizione.

Fine.

Fine.

TRIO.

94

RONDO.
Allegro ma non troppo.

Allegro ma non troppo.

Violin Sonata No. 6 in A Major

OP. 30, NO. 1

110   *Violin Sonata No. 6*

114   *Violin Sonata No. 6*

Allegretto con Variazioni.

VAR.I.

VAR.VI.
Allegro, ma non tanto.

Allegro, ma non tanto.

Violin Sonata No. 7 in C Minor

OP. 30, NO. 2

126   *Violin Sonata No. 7*

SCHERZO.

Allegro.

TRIO.

FINALE.
Allegro.

Violin Sonata No. 8 in G Major

OP. 30, NO. 3

Tempo di Minuetto.
ma molto moderato e grazioso.

172   Violin Sonata No. 8

Violin Sonata No. 9 in A Minor ("Kreutzer")

OP. 47

VAR.I.

sempre piano

FINALE.
Presto.

202   *Violin Sonata No. 9*

208 *Violin Sonata No. 9*

Violin Sonata No. 10 in G Major

OP. 96

SCHERZO.
Allegro.

CODA.

228   *Violin Sonata No. 10*